The Brainbox Quiz Book

BEANObooks
geddes & grosset

Calling all you Brainboxes!
Get your brain in gear and
see how well you do
answering the questions in
this brand new Brainbox
Quizbook.

Each page has 10
questions - one on each of
the subjects shown on the
page opposite.

At the end of
each page, jot
down how many
correct answers you
get and be amazed at
what a smarty
pants you are!

Topics

Numbers

Countries

Animals

Food & Drink

Books

History

Spelling

Music

People

Lucky Dip

3

Numbers

1. How many thieves did Ali Baba meet?

Countries

2. In which country would you find the Eiffel Tower?

Animals

3. What kind of a creature is a grayling?

Food & Drink

4. Ravioli is a type of what?

Books

5. Who wrote The Famous Five books?

History

6. Who was the father of Elizabeth I?

Spelling

7. One of these three spellings is correct. Which one is it? stammina; staminna; stamina.

Music

8. Which Beatle sang Yellow Submarine?

People

9. Who or what was a Tsar?

Lucky Dip

10. In the film E.T., what do the initials stand for?

Answers

1.Forty. 2.France. 3.A fish. 4.Pasta. 5.Enid Blyton. 6.Henry VIII. 7.Stamina. 8.Ringo Starr. 9.A Russian emperor. 10.Extra-terrestrial.

Numbers

1. How many days are there in a leap year?

Countries

2. By what name is Eire also known?

Animals

3. What is the name of a female fox?

Food & Drink

4. Earl Grey is a type of which drink?

Books

5. In which book would you find the character Ratty?

History

6. Which recent film told the story of Scotland's William Wallace?

Spelling

7. Which is the correct spelling? colandar; colendar; colander?

Music

8. On which instrument would you find a chanter?

People

9. Nelson Mandela was born in which country?

Lucky Dip

10. Who lives in The Vatican?

Answers

1.Three hundred and sixty six. 2.Ireland. 3.A vixen. 4.Tea. 5.The Wind in the Willows. 6.Braveheart. 7.Colander. 8.The Bagpipes. 9.South Africa. 10.The Pope.

Numbers

1. How many sides are in a hexagon?

Countries

2. What is the capital of Sweden?

Animals

3. In The Jungle Book, what kind of animal is Shere Khan?

Food & Drink

4. Stilton is a type of what food?

Books

5. The film Hook continues the story of which book?

History

6. How did Mary, Queen of Scots die?

Spelling

7. Which is the correct spelling? macaronni, macaroni, macarroni?

Music

8. Who had a hit with the song "Let me entertain you"?

People

9. What is the name of Dennis the Menace's little sister?

Lucky Dip

10. What was the name of the ship which sank after hitting an iceberg in 1912?

Answers

1.Six. 2.Stockholm. 3.A tiger. 4.Cheese. 5.Peter Pan. 6.She was beheaded. 7.Macaroni. 8.Robbie Williams. 9.Bea. 10.The Titanic.

Numbers

1. How many dwarfs are there in the Snow White story?

Countries

2. If you were in the city of Madrid, which country would you be in?

Animals

3. What can Dr Doolittle do with animals?

Food & Drink

4. What is a humbug?

Books

5. Who wrote The Very Hungry Caterpillar?

History

6. Who tried to blow up Parliament with gunpowder?

Spelling

7. What is the correct spelling? orchestra, orkestra, orchistra?

Music

8. In which musical would you find Macavity the cat?

People

9. By what name is Reginald Dwight better known?

Lucky Dip

10. In the nursery rhyme, what did the cow jump over?

Answers

1. Seven. 2. Spain. 3. Talk to them. 4. A boiled sweet. 5. Eric Carle. 6. Guy Fawkes. 7. Orchestra. 8. Cats. 9. Sir Elton John. 10. The moon.

11

Numbers

1. In Roman numerals, what does the letter X stand for?

Countries

2. Brazil is the largest country in South America. True or false?

Animals

3. Sumatran, Bengal and Indian are all types of which?

Food & Drink

4. What is the main ingredient of coleslaw?

Books

5. In which book would you find the character Bill Sykes?

History

6. What year was Queen Elizabeth II crowned?

Spelling

7. What is the correct spelling?
mantlepiece;
mantelpeace;
mantelpiece?

Music

8. Who sang the theme tune from Bob the Builder?

People

9. Who "went to sea in a beautiful pea green boat"?

Lucky Dip

10. What colours would you mix together to get green?

Answers

10.Blue and yellow.
7.Mantelpiece. 8.Neil Morrisey. 9.The owl and the pussy-cat.
1.Ten. 2.True. 3.Tiger. 4.Cabbage. 5.Oliver Twist. 6.1953.

13

Numbers

1. What is the sixth letter of the alphabet?

Countries

2. Which ocean is between Britain and America?

Animals

3. A dromedary is a type of what?

Food & Drink

4. What is paella?

Books

5. Who wrote Lord of the Rings?

History

6. Which Scottish town was made a city in 2001?

Spelling

7. What is the correct spelling - magishian; magicion; magician?

Music

8. The song "Waltzing Matilda" comes from which country?

People

9. Name the present American president.

Lucky Dip

10. What are jodphurs?

Answers

1.F. 2.Atlantic. 3.A camel. 4.A Spanish dish made from rice and seafood. 5.JR Tolkien. 6.Inverness. 7.Magician. 8.Australia. 9.George W Bush. 10.Riding breeches.

Numbers

1. How many cakes would you have if you bought one and a quarter dozen?

Countries

2. Where would you find EuroDisney?

Animals

3. Siamese, Persian and Burmese are all types of what?

Food & Drink

4. What is a pomegranate?

Books

5. In which book would you find Aslan?

History

6. Who first discovered Australia?

Spelling

7. What is the correct spelling - occasion; ocassion; occassion?

Music

8. The song the "Yellow Brick Road" comes from which film?

People

9. What is the name of Bart Simpson's dad?

Lucky Dip

10. What is Quidditch?

Answers

1. Fifteen. 2. Paris. 3. Cats. 4. A fruit. 5. The Lion The Witch and the Wardrobe. 6. Captain James Cook. 7. Occasion. 8. The Wizard of Oz. 9. Homer. 10. A game played at Harry Potter's school, Hogwarts.

Numbers

1. On a dice, what is on the opposite side from six?

Countries

2. The drachma was the currency of which country?

Animals

3. In Winnie the Pooh, what kind of animal is Eeyore?

Food & Drink

4. Junket is a type of milk pudding. True or false?

Books

5. Who wrote James and the Giant Peach?

History

6. What were The Suffragettes?

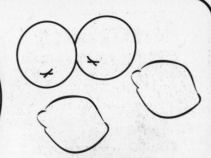

Spelling

7. What is the correct spelling - paraffin; parrafin; pareffin.

Music

8. 'Oranges and lemons, say the bells of St ...."?

People

9. What is a Sassenach?

Lucky Dip

10. Who lives in The White House?

Answers

1.One. 2.Greece. 3.A donkey. 4.True. 5.Roald Dahl. 6.In the early twentieth century women who demanded the right to vote. 7.Paraffin. 8.Clements. 9.A Scottish term for an English person. 10.The president of the USA.

Numbers

1. How many are in a trilogy?

Countries

2. What is the capital of Southern Ireland?

Animals

3. What is a bottlenose?

Food & Drink

4. What is a tortilla?

Books

5. In which book will you find Pongo and Perdita?

History

6. Who were also known as The Magi?

Spelling

7. What is the correct spelling - computar; computer; computor?

Music

8. In which country was Britney Spears born?

People

9. What do you call someone who lives in Manchester?

Lucky Dip

10. What is shinty?

Answers

1.Three. 2.Dublin. 3.A type of dolphin. 4.A Mexican flatbread. 5.101 Dalmatians. 6.The Three Wise Men. 7.Computer. 8.America. 9.A Mancunian. 10.A game played in Scotland.

Numbers

1. How many players are there in a polo team?

Countries

2. In which country would you find the Table Mountain?

Animals

3. What is a Dandy Dinmont?

Food & Drink

4. If you bought a cappuccino, what would you be drinking?

Books

5. Complete the following book title:- Charlie and the ....

History

6. What is the name of the wall which the Romans built between Scotland and England?

Spelling

7. What is the correct spelling:- pantomine; pantamime; pantomime?

Music

8. If you had a zither, would you beat it, blow it, or pluck it?

People

9. What is Madonna's full name?

Lucky Dip

10. Euston, King's Cross and Waverley are all types of what?

Answers 1.Four. 2.South Africa. 3.A breed of dog. 4.A coffee. 5.Charlie and the Chocolate Factory. 6.Hadrian's Wall. 7.Pantomime. 8.You would pluck it - it's a stringed instrument! 9.Madonna Louise Veronica Ciccone. 10.Railway Stations.

Numbers

1. How many Spice Girls were there originally?

Countries

2. The River Liffey runs through which European capital?

Animals

3. What is the name for a group of lions?

Food & Drink

4. Clementine, satsuma, Granny Smith. What is the odd one out?

Books

5. In which book would you find Mowgli?

History

6. How many years was Queen Victoria on the throne?

Spelling

7. What is the correct spelling:-
coconut:
cocoanut:
coaconut?

Music

8. Which group sang the song Bohemian Rhapsody?

People

9. By what name is Jamie Oliver also known?

Lucky Dip

10. Madame Tussauds is famous for what?

Answers

1.Five. 2.Dublin. 3.Pride. 4.Granny Smith (the other two are citrus fruits). 5.Jungle Book. 6.64 years. 7.Coconut. 8.Queen. 9.The Naked Chef. 10.Waxwork models.

Numbers

1. How many years are in half a century?

Countries

2. If you heard someone yodelling, which country might you be in?

Animals

3. A Falabella is the smallest breed of which animal?

Food & Drink

4. What is Desperate Dan's favourite food?

Books

5. What was the name of the tiny people Gulliver met on his travels?

History

6. The Great Fire of London started in Pudding Lane. true or false?

Spelling

7. What is the correct spelling - conscious; conscous; concious?

Music

8. What do the initials CD stand for?

People

9. What is Prince William's full name?

Lucky Dip

10. In the nursery rhyme what did Tom, Tom, the piper's son steal?

Answers

1.Fifty. 2.Switzerland. 3.Horse. 4.Cow Pie. 5.Lilliputians. 6.True. 7.Conscious. 8.Compact Disc. 9.William Arthur Philip Louis Windsor. 10.A pig.

Numbers

1. How many months have just 30 days in them?

Countries

2. Vienna is the capital of which country?

Animals

3. Who has a dog called Gnasher?

Food & Drink

4. What kind of food is Edam?

Books

5. In which books would you find Huckleberry Finn?

History

6. Who was Dick Turpin?

Spelling

7. What is the correct spelling - spagettie; spaghetti; spaggheti?

Music

8. Who is the lead singer with The Rolling Stones?

People

9. What is the Queen's daughter called?

Lucky Dip

10. What was unusual about the film "Bugsy Malone"?

Answers

1.Four. 2.Austria. 3.Dennis the Menace. 4.Cheese. 5.The Adventures of Tom Sawyer and Huckleberry Finn. 6.A famous highwayman. 7.Spaghetti. 8.Mick Jagger. 9.Anne. 10.All the parts were played by children.

Numbers

1. In Roman numerals, what does the letter C stand for?

Countries

2. What colours are the Scottish flag?

Animals

3. What is a Lhasa Apso?

Food & Drink

4. What is Popeye's favourite food?

Books

5. In which book would you find The Mad Hatter?

History

6. Which French Queen was sent to the guillotine?

Spelling

7. What is the correct spelling- decieve; deceive; deceeve?

Music

8. What is a plectrum?

People

9. Who directed the films ET., Jurassic Park, and Hook among others?

Lucky Dip

10. Which school house did Harry Potter join?

Answers

1.One hundred. 2.Blue with a white cross. 3.A breed of dog. 4.Spinach. 5.Alice in Wonderland. 6.Marie-Antoinette. 7.Deceive. 8.A small device for plucking guitar strings. 9.Steven Spielberg. 10.Gryffindor.

Numbers

1. How many continents are there?

Countries

2. Which country was originally called Persia?

Animals

3. Which Scottish loch is home to a famous monster?

Food & Drink

4. Which bear loved marmalade sandwiches?

Books

5. Who wrote James and the Giant Peach?

History

6. How did the Titanic sink?

Spelling

7. What is the correct spelling- secretary; secretery, secritary?

Music

8. Who wrote "Mull of Kintyre"?

People

9. With which sport do you associate Jensen Button?

Lucky Dip

10. Which cartoon characters live in Bedrock?

Answers

1.Five. 2.Iran. 3.Loch Ness. 4.Paddington. 5.Roald Dahl. 6.It hit a huge ice-berg. 7.Secretary. 8.Paul McCartney. 9.Motor racing. 10.The Flintstones.

Numbers

1. What is ten per cent of 150?

Countries

2. What are the Outer Hebrides?

Animals

3. What is a baby goose called?

Food & Drink

4. What is the main ingredient of porridge?

Books

5. Who wrote Fungus the Bogeyman?

History

6. What was the name of Captain Scott's ship?

Spelling

7. What is the correct spelling- advocado; avacado; avocado?

Music

8. In The Muppets, which instrument did Animal play?

People

9. Inuits are also known as what?

Lucky Dip

10. In which sport would you find a conversion?

Answers

1.Fifteen. 2.Islands off the coast of Scotland. 3.Gosling. 4.Oatmeal. 5.Raymond Briggs. 6.The Discovery. 7.Avocado. 8.Drums. 9.Eskimos. 10.Rugby.

35

Numbers

1. In the nursery rhyme how many fiddlers did Old King Cole call for?

Countries

2. In which country would you find The Kremlin?

Animals

3. Which lizard can change colour to suit its surroundings?

Food & Drink

4. What is a cob?

Books

5. In which book would you find Mary Lennox?

History

6. During which years was the Second World War fought?

Spelling

7. What is the correct spelling - parsley: parssley; parsly?

Music

8. From which musical does the song "It's a Hard Knock Life" come?

People

9. With which sport do you associate Lennox Lewis?

Lucky Dip

10. Finish the following saying. The early bird catches ... .

Answers

1.Three. 2.Russia. 3.Chameleon. 4.A loaf of bread. 5.The Secret Garden. 6.1939/1945. 7.Parsley. 8.Annie. 9.Boxing. 10.The worm.

Numbers

1. How many 2p stamps do you get in a dozen?

Countries

2. Which country celebrates Thanksgiving Day in November?

Animals

3. What is the correct name for the American buffalo?

Food & Drink

4. What is the main ingredient of marzipan?

Books

5. What are the names of Harry Potter's parents?

History

6. Which is Scotland's oldest university?

Spelling

7. What is the correct spelling - antilope; antalope; antelope?

Music

8. Which group sang the song "Waterloo"?

People

9. George W Bush's father was also a president of the USA. True or false?

Lucky Dip

10. Bronze is a metal made out of copper and which other metal?

Answers

1.A dozen! 2.America. 3.The Bison. 4.Ground almonds. 5.James and Lily. 6.St. Andrews. 7.Antelope. 8.Abba. 9.True. 10.Tin.

Numbers

1. If you have £3.75 and spend £1.19 how much is left?

Countries

2. Is Antarctica in the Northern or Southern Hemisphere?

Animals

3. Would you find a Dugong in water or on land?

Food & Drink

4. What is an anchovy?

Books

5. Who wrote The Wind in the Willows?

History

6. Who was the first explorer to sail around the world?

Spelling

7. What is the correct spelling - cockatto; cockattoo; cockatoo?

Music

8. What kind of musical instrument is played in churches?

People

9. Who played Edmund Blackadder in the tv series?

Lucky Dip

10. Where is the Sea of Tranquillity?

Answers

1. £2.56. 2. Southern. 3. In water. It's a whale-like mammal. 4. A small member of the herring family. 5. Kenneth T. Grahame. 6. Magellan. 7. Cockatoo. 8. The organ. 9. Rowan Atkinson. 10. The Moon.

Numbers

1. Seven months of the year have 31 days. How many have 28?

Countries

2. In which country did the dog the Great Dane, originate?

Animals

3. What kind of animal is a marsupial?

Food & Drink

4. What is a knickerbocker glory?

Books

5. Complete the title- The Prince and ... .?

History

6. What was the name of Queen Victoria's husband?

DRUM! DRUM! DRUM! DRUM!

Spelling

7. What is the correct spelling - calendar; callendar; calender?

Music

8. What song was written for the Band Aid relief project?

People

9. Who was the star of the film Gladiator?

Lucky Dip

10. Which superhero was known as Clark Kent?

Answers

1.They all do! 2.Germany. 3.One which carries its young in a pouch. 4.A fabulous dish of ice cream, raspberry sauce, chocolate and cream! 5.The Pauper. 6.Prince Albert. 7.Calendar. 8.Do They Know It's Christmas? 9.Russell Crowe. 10.Superman.

43

Numbers

1. On what date is April Fool's Day?

Countries

2. How many states make up The United States of America?

Animals

3. Who created Mickey Mouse?

Food & Drink

4. Which fruit is traditionally served in a sauce with roast turkey?

Books

5. By what name was Lord Greystokes better known?

History

6. When did the 2nd World War begin?

Spelling

7. What is the correct spelling - jewellery; jewellry; jewelery?

Music

8. Who sang with Robbie Williams on the hit "Something Stupid"?

People

9. Who played the title role in the recent film "Dr. Dolittle"?

Lucky Dip

10. Eoraptor is one of the oldest known what?

Answers

1.April 1st. 2.50. 3.Walt Disney. 4.Cranberry. 5.Tarzan. 6.1939. 7.Jewellery. 8.Nicole Kidman. 9.Eddie Murphy. 10.Dinosaur.

Numbers

1. What kind of clock has a bird which pops out and sings every hour?

Countries

2. What is the largest ocean in the world?

Animals

3. What is a baby goat called?

Food & Drink

4. If you had a sarsparilla, what would you do with it?

Books

5. Complete the following book title:- Swallows And ....

History

6. In what year did Scotland get her own parliament?

Spelling

7. What is the correct spelling - sandal; sandall; sandel?

Music

8. Who sang the theme song in the film of The Lion King?

People

9. For what was Pablo Picasso famous?

Lucky Dip

10. Which island is associated with the Manx cat?

Answers

1.Cuckoo. 2.Pacific. 3.Kid. 4.Drink it! 5.Amazons. 6.1999. 7.Sandal. 8.Sir Elton John. 9.Painting. 10.Isle of Man.

Numbers

1. How long does the Earth take to orbit the sun?

Countries

2. Penguins can be found in the Arctic. True or false?

Animals

3. What is a nocturnal animal?

Food & Drink

4. Gazpacho is a type of Spanish soup. What is different about it?

Books

5. In which street did the famous detective Sherlock Holmes live?

History

6. Who became the first black president of South Africa?

Spelling

7. What is the correct spelling - Propellor; Propelor; Propeller?

Music

8. Finish this famous song title "Don't Cry For Me ....?

People

9. Whose nose grew longer every time he told a lie?

Lucky Dip

10. Which game has Knights and Bishops?

Answers

1. Just over three hundred and sixty five days. 2. False. 3. One which hunts at night. 4. It is served cold. 5. Baker Street. 6. Nelson Mandela. 7. Propeller. 8. Argentina. 9. Pinocchio. 10. Chess.

Numbers

1. How many metres are in a kilometre?

Countries

2. Which country is often referred to as The Emerald Isle?

Animals

3. What is a Maine Coon?

Food & Drink

4. Pilau and Basmati are types of what?

Books

5. Who, in the fairy tale, wore a glass slipper?

History

6. Which country was defeated by the British at the Battle of Waterloo?

Spelling

7. What is the correct spelling- marmilade; marmelade; marmalade?

Music

8. In music, what does the term forte mean?

People

9. Which fictional superhero lives in Metropolis?

Lucky Dip

10. What is the main ingredient of glass?

Answers

9.Superman. 10.Sand.
5.Cinderella. 6.France. 7.Marmalade. 8.Loud.
1.One thousand. 2.Ireland. 3.A breed of cat. 4.Rice.

51

Numbers

1. How many of each animal did Noah take into the Ark?

Countries

2. Which city is overlooked by the Sugar Loaf Mountain?

Animals

3. From which country does the Kookaburra come?

Food & Drink

4. What is a naan?

Books

5. Which Christmas story features Ebeneezer Scrooge?

History

6. What form of transport did the early settlers use to cross America?

Spelling

7. What is the correct spelling -sergent; sergeant; sargeant?

Music

8. "You're The One That I Want" featured in which musical film?

People

9. For what was John Constable famous?

Lucky Dip

10. Where does cork come from?

Answers

1.Two. 2.Rio de Janeiro. 3.Australia. 4.Indian bread. 5.A Christmas Carol. 6.Horse-drawn wagons. 7.Sergeant. 8.Grease. 9.Landscape paintings. 10.The bark of the cork tree.

53

Numbers

1. How many minutes does a football match last?

Countries

2. Which river runs through the Grand Canyon?

Animals

3. The word hippopotamus stands for river horse - true or false?

Food & Drink

4. Does ginger come from seeds or a root?

Books

5. Who wrote "A Christmas Carol"?

History

6. Queen Victoria reigned during two centuries. Which?

Spelling

7. What is the correct spelling-conjuror; conjiror; conjurur?

Music

8. Who sang the theme song from the film The Snowman?

People

9. What does a geologist study?

Lucky Dip

10. Which one of the following isn't a sign of the zodiac - Leo, Aries, Pluto?

Answers

1.Ninety. 2.The Colorado. 3.True. 4.A root. 5.Charles Dickens. 6.19th and 20th. 7.Conjuror. 8.Aled Jones. 9.The structure and composition of the Earth. 10.Pluto.

Numbers

1. How many sides does an octagon have?

Countries

2. Which is the largest continent in the world?

Animals

3. Which bird is the national emblem of the USA?

Food & Drink

4. Is coffee made from beans or leaves?

Books

5. What is a book of maps called?

History

6. Which British king gave up his throne in 1936?

Spelling

7. What is the correct spelling - dinosaur; dinosoar; dinosore?

Music

8. Which is the odd one out flute, clarinet, cymbals?

People

9. Who played Han Solo in the first three Star Wars films?

Lucky Dip

10. Does a north wind blow in a southerly or northernly direction?

Answers

1.Eight. 2.Asia. 3.The Bald Eagle. 4.Beans. 5.An Atlas. 6.Edward the VIII. 7.Dinosaur. 8.Cymbals - the other two are wind instruments. 9.Harrison Ford. 10.Southerly!

Numbers

1. The number 2002 is a palindrome. What is a palindrome?

Countries

2. Lisbon is the capital city of which country?

Animals

3. What is a dingo?

Food & Drink

4. The Americans call them cookies. What are they called in Britain?

Books

5. Who lives in The Hundred Acre Wood?

History

6. Who were Bonnie and Clyde?

Spelling

7. What is the correct spelling - aquariam; aquariem; aquarium?

Music

8. In which Musical would you find a character called Eponine?

People

9. With which sport do you associate Matthew Pinsett?

Lucky Dip

10. What is a carnivore?

Answers

1. A number or word which can be read the same forwards as backwards. 2. Portugal. 3. A wild Australian dog. 4. Biscuits. 5. Winnie the Pooh and friends. 6. American bank robbers. 7. Aquarium. 8. Les Miserables. 9. Rowing. 10. A meat eater.

Numbers

1. How many people perform in a duet?

Countries

2. With which country do you associate windmills?

Animals

3. Can hens fly?

Food & Drink

4. What is a Victoria sandwich?

Books

5. Who wrote The Little Mermaid?

History

6. Which explorer sailed in The Endurance?

Spelling

7. What is the correct spelling-
vaccinate:
vacinnate:
vaccanate?

Music

8. What is a soprano?

People

9. What is the name of the Queen's husband?

Lucky Dip

10. What is a bantam?

Answers 1.Two. 2.Holland. 3.Short distances - if they have to. 4.A sponge cake. 5.Hans Christian Andersen. 6.Sir Ernest Shackleton. 7.Vaccinate. 8.The highest variety of singing voice. 9.Philip. 10.A small variety of hen.

Numbers

1. In the song "Twelve Days of Christmas" what does "my true love" give on the 5th day?

Countries

2. In which country would you find The Champs Elysee?

Animals

3. What happens to garden snails in winter?

Food & Drink

4. Cayenne is a type of what?

Books

5. Who wrote The Borrowers books?

History

6. What is special about American Neil Armstrong?

Spelling

7. What is the correct spelling - apostriphe: appostrophe; apostrophe?

Music

8. What nationality is Kylie Minogue?

People

9. Caspar, Balthazar and Melchior were all - what?

Lucky Dip

10. Marshmallows were originally made from the root of the marshmallow plant. True or false?

Answers

1.Five gold rings. 2.Paris, France. 3.They hibernate. 4.Pepper. 5.Mary Norton. 6.He was the first man to walk on the moon. 7.Apostrophe. 8.Australian. 9.The Three Wise Men. 10.True.

Numbers

1. How many members were in The Beatles?

Countries

2. Which country is south of Canada?

Animals

3. What is a Red Kite?

Food & Drink

4. What is Cockaleekie?

Books

5. Who was Noddy's best friend?

History

6. Of which country was Robert the Bruce king?

Spelling

7. What is the correct spelling - mistletoe; misteltoe; misseltoe?

Music

8. Is a lament happy or sad?

People

9. Chief Crazy Horse and General Custer fought at which battle?

Lucky Dip

10. What sport is played at Wimbledon?

Answers

1.Four. 2.The United States of America. 3.A bird. 4.A soup. 5.Big Ears. 6.Scotland. 7.Mistletoe. 8.Sad. 9.Little Big Horn. 10.Tennis.

Numbers

1. What was the code number used by James Bond?

Countries

2. In which continent is Greece?

Animals

3. Is a whale a fish or a mammal?

Food & Drink

4. Where did the first potatoes grow?

Books

5. Which train did Harry Potter catch to school?

History

6. Which king tried to turn back the sea?

Spelling

7. What is the correct spelling -decieve; deseive; deceive?

Music

8. "Oh, say can you see, by the dawn's early light"? are the opening lines of which National Anthem?

People

9. What is the name of Tony and Cherie Blair's youngest child?

Lucky Dip

10. What travels at the speed of knots?

Answers

8.The American. 9.Leo. 10.Ships
6.King Canute. 7.Deceive.
1.007. 2.Europe. 3.Mammal. 4.America. 5.Hogwart Express.

Numbers

1. How many wonders of the world were there?

Countries

2. Which countries are separated by the Pyrenees?

Animals

3. What breed of dog is associated with the Queen?

Food & Drink

4. Which vitamin do we get from citrus fruits?

Books

5. Who was given a poisoned apple by her step-mother?

History

6. Who led a herd of elephants across the Alps?

Spelling

7. What is the correct spelling - monastry; monastary; monastery?

Music

8. Which pop group features the Gallacher brothers?

People

9. Rudolph Nureyev was a famous musician. True or False?

Lucky Dip

10. How many reindeer does Santa Claus have?

Answers

1.Seven. 2.France and Spain. 3.Corgi. 4.Vitamin C. 5.Snow White. 6.Hannibal. 7.Monastery. 8.Oasis. 9.False. He was a ballet dancer. 10.Nine.

Numbers

1. Is the next leap year in 2004 or 2006?

Countries

2. The Rand is the currency of which country?

Animals

3. Which animals did the Pied Piper drive from Hamelin?

Food & Drink

4. Apart from tea, what else is in Russian tea?

Books

5. In which country is the story of Heidi set?

History

6. Good King Wenceslas was king of which country?

Spelling

7. What is the correct spelling - squirrel; squirel; squirell?

Music

8. In the musical Annie, what is the name of her little dog?

People

9. For what is John Logie Baird famous?

Lucky Dip

10. What creature would you find in an aviary?

Answers
1.Two thousand and four. 2.South Africa. 3.Rats. 4.Lemon. 5.Switzerland. 6.Bohemia. 7.Squirrel. 8.Sandy. 9.He invented television. 10.Birds.

71

Numbers

1. Who lives at No.10 Downing Street?

Countries

2. In which country would you ride in a gondola?

Animals

3. Which is the fastest land animal?

Food & Drink

4. Eccles, Fruit and Battenberg are all types of which?

Books

5. Who wrote Pride and Prejudice?

History

6. Which American president was shot in Dallas, Texas?

Music

8. Who was the lead singer with the Boomtown Rats?

Spelling

7. What is the correct spelling - prosess; process; proccess?

People

9. Marco Polo was an explorer. True or False.

Lucky Dip

10. Ming the Merciless was whose enemy?

Answers

1.The Prime Minister. 2.Italy. 3.Cheetah. 4.Cakes. 5.Jane Austen. 6.John F. Kennedy. 7.Process. 8.Bob Geldof. 9.True. 10.Flash Gordon.

Numbers

1. Which two letters are worth 10 points in the game of Scrabble?

Countries

2. What is the capital of Poland?

Animals

3. Which creatures live in a formicary?

Food & Drink

4. Shortcrust, flaky and rough puff are all types of what?

Books

5. Which fictional creatures lived on Wimbledon Common?

History

6. What famous Dogs' Home was founded in 1871?

Spelling

7. What is the correct spelling - amazeing; amazing; amayzing?

Music

8. Complete the first line of this song. A spoonful of sugar ....

People

9. Who has a son called Brooklyn?

Lucky Dip

10. What colour is a New York taxi?

Answers

1.Q and Z. 2.Warsaw. 3.Ants. 4.Pastry. 5.The Wombles. 6.Battersea. 7. Amazing. 8.Makes the medicine go down. 9.David and Victoria Beckham. 10.Yellow.

Numbers

1. What number would you divide 49 by to get 7?

Countries

2. King Juan Carlos is King of which country?

Animals

3. What is a black widow?

Food & Drink

4. What type of cheese is usually found on a pizza?

Books

5. In the novel, who or what was Moby Dick?

History

6. In which century did the first motor car appear?

Spelling

7. What is the correct spelling - pasttime; pastime; passtime?

Music

8. Which instrument are angels reputed to play?

People

9. By what name is Robin of Locksley better known?

Lucky Dip

10. Which games are played with a cue?

Answers

1.Seven! 2.Spain. 3.A spider. 4.Mozarella. 5.A whale. 6.The 19th. 7.Pastime. 8.Harps. 9.Robin Hood. 10.Snooker, billiards and pool.

Numbers

1. What do the Roman numerals XIX stand for?

Countries

2. The four countries of Denmark, Sweden, Norway and Finland are otherwise known collectively as what?

Animals

3. Which bird has the longest wingspan in the world?

Food & Drink

4. In cooking, what does the term puree, mean?

Books

5. Matthew, Mark, Luke and John are known as the Books of what?

History

6. Which glen in Scotland was the scene of a massacre in the 16th century?

Spelling

7. What is the correct spelling - torpedoes; torpeedoes; torrpedoes?

Music

8. From which country did the group Abba come?

People

9. Which actor played the lead in the film Forrest Gump?

Lucky Dip

10. What do the initials M.B.E. stand for?

Answers

1.Nineteen. 2.Scandinavia. 3.The wandering albatross. 4.Food which has been sieved or pulped. 5.The Gospel. 6.Glencoe. 7.Torpedoes. 8.Sweden. 9.Tom Hanks. 10.Member of the British Empire.

Numbers

1. How many people are in a quartet?

Countries

2. The Sahara is the world's largest desert. Where would you find it?

Animals

3. Which insect shares its name with a sport?

Food & Drink

4. Korma, tandoori and vindaloo are all which kinds of food?

Books

5. What is the name of the owl in the Harry Potter books?

History

6. Which explorer and his team perished at the South Pole at the beginning of the 20th century?

Spelling

7. What is the correct spelling - sandwitch: sangwich; sandwich?

People

9. By what name is Mrs David Beckham better known?

Music

8. Ronan Keating was the lead singer of which group?

Lucky Dip

10. What does the text message BCNU mean?

Answers

1.Four. 2.North Africa. 3.Cricket. 4.Indian. 5.Hedwig. 6.Captain Scott. 7.Sandwich. 8.Boyzone. 9.Posh Spice. 10.Be seeing you.

Numbers

1. Complete the following sum:- 12 x 2 = 24 - ? =16

Countries

2. What is the largest island in the world?

Animals

3. Which bird lays its eggs in other bird's nests?

Food & Drink

4. What is grown in paddy fields?

Books

5. In which book would you find Meg, Jo, Beth and Amy?

History

6. Which country attacked the American navy at Pearl Harbour?

Spelling

7. What is the correct spelling - thisteldown; thisseldown; thistledown?

Music

8. 'God Save the Queen' is Britain's National what?

People

9. Who is the host of tv's Blind Date programme?

Lucky Dip

10. What is a Blue Peter?

Answers

1.Eight. 2.Greenland. 3.The Cuckoo. 4.Rice. 5.Little Women 6.Japan. 7.Thistledown. 8.Anthem. 9.Cilla Black. 10.A flag which a ship hoists when it is about to sail.

Numbers

1. What is the first letter of the Greek Alphabet?

Countries

2. Which country has a maple leaf on its flag?

Animals

3. Which is the only insect which provides food fit for humans?

Food & Drink

4. What type of food is a plantain?

Books

5. What was Cinderella's coach made from?

History

6. Of which country was Cleopatra Queen?

Spelling

7. What is the correct spelling - Abysinnia; Abisinnia; Abyssinia?

Music

8. What kind of instruments would you find in the percussion section of an orchestra?

People

9. Of which religion is the Dalai Lama the leader?

Lucky Dip

10. In Mediaeval times, what were Court Jesters?

Answers

1.Alpha. 2.Canada. 3.The Bee! (Honey) 4.Banana. 5.A pumpkin. 6.Egypt. 7.Abyssinia. 8.Drums, cymbals, etc. 9.The Buddhist. 10.Entertainers.

Numbers

1. How often does a leap year occur?

Countries

2. Between which two countries is the world's longest border?

Animals

3. From which animal do we get mohair wool?

Food & Drink

4. Haricot, runner and broad are all types of what?

Books

5. In which books would you find Gandalf?

History

6. Which King had his court at Camelot?

Spelling

7. What is the correct spelling- heavenly; hevenly; heavenley?

Music

8. Where did reggae music originate?

People

9. With what sport is Michael Jordan associated?

Lucky Dip

10. Do snakes have bones?

Answers

1. Every 4 years. 2. Canada and the United States. 3. Angora goat. 4. Beans. 5. The Lord of the Rings. 6. Arthur. 7. Heavenly. 8. Jamaica. 9. Basketball. 10. Yes, lots of them!

Numbers

1. Which planet has 18 moons?

Countries

2. Which river is spanned by the longest suspension bridge in the British Isles?

Animals

3. Which are the most intelligent of all sea mammals?

Food & Drink

4. What do you put in a percolator?

Books

5. Who had a dog called Toto?

History

6. In which country was the Ming Dynasty?

Spelling

7. What is the correct spelling - fantom, phantam; phantom?

Music

8. What does the musical term adagio, mean?

People

9. What part of the body does a chiropodist deal with?

Lucky Dip

10. Name the longest running pop programme on British television.

Answers

1. Saturn. 2. The Humber. 3. Dolphins. 4. Coffee. 5. Dorothy in the Wizard of Oz. 6. China. 7. Phantom. 8. Slowly. 9. The feet. 10. Top of the Pops.

Numbers

1. How many are in a score?

Countries

2. How many countries make up The British Isles?

Animals

3. What is a female elephant called?

Food & Drink

4. What is dhal?

Books

5. Which famous book did Dodie Smith write?

History

6. In what year was President Kennedy assassinated?

Spelling

7. What is the correct spelling - artificial; artificiel; artafacial?

Music

8. Complete the following song title "Lucy in the sky ...."

People

9. What are Siamese twins?

Lucky Dip

10. How many colours are in the rainbow?

Answers 1.Twenty. 2.Four. Scotland, England, Northern Ireland and Wales. 3.A cow. 4.An Indian dish made from lentils. 5.101 Dalmatians. 6.1963. 7.Artificial. 8.With diamonds. 9.Twins which are born joined together. 10.Seven. Red, orange, yellow, green, blue, indigo and violet.

Numbers

1. How many cards are in a pack of playing cards?

Countries

2. In which country is Zeebrugge?

Animals

3. What is the strongest creature in the world?

Food & Drink

4. Basil, oregano and thyme are all types of what?

Books

5. Who wrote "Maurice and his Educated Rodents"?

History

6. Which ancient Egyptian monarch was known as The Boy King?

Spelling

7. What is the correct spelling - camoflage; camouflage; camofflage?

Music

8. In music, what do the initials C&W stand for?

People

9. Name the explorer who brought tobacco and potatoes to Britain.

Lucky Dip

10. In which film would you find Woody and Buzz Lightyear?

Answers

1.Fifty two. 2.Belgium. 3.The Rhinoceros Beetle! 4.Herbs.
5.Terry Pratchett. 6.Tutankhamun. 7.Camouflage.
8.Country and Western.
9.Sir Walter Raleigh. 10.Toy Story.

Numbers

1. For how many years did Sleeping Beauty actually sleep?

Countries

2. In which country would you find the Pennines?

Animals

3. In the cartoon series "Tom and Jerry" what type of creature is Jerry?

Food & Drink

4. What drink would you get from a samovar?

Books

5. In which book would you find Humpty Dumpty?

History

6. Which English king had six wives?

Spelling

7. What is the correct spelling: endeavor; endevour; endeavour?

Music

8. A viola is a member of the violin family. True or False?

People

9. Where in London would you find The Beefeaters?

Lucky Dip

10. Which famous comic character lives in Cactusville?

Answers

1. One hundred years. 2. England. 3. A mouse! 4. Tea. It's a Russian tea urn. 5. Through the Looking Glass. 6. Henry the Eighth. 7. Endeavour. 8. True. 9. Guarding The Tower of London. 10. Desperate Dan.

95

Well, how did you score?

0-4 on each page – it's time to pay more attention in school!

5-7 – pretty impressive!

8-10 – go straight to the top of the class!